SHAPED BY THE BIBLE

William H. Willimon

ABINGDON PRESS
Nashville

SHAPED BY THE BIBLE

Copyright © 1990 by Abingdon Press

This book is printed on acid-free paper.

Library of Congress Cataloging-in-Publication Data

WILLIMON, WILLIAM H.
    Shaped by the Bible / William H. Willimon.
        p.   cm. — (Faithful congregations series)
    ISBN 0-687-12656-8 (alk. paper)
        1. Church. 2. Bible—Influence. I. Title II. Series.
    BV600.2.W545   1990
    262—dc20   90-21921
                                                                      CIP

*Scripture quotations are from the New Revised Standard Version of the Bible,
copyright 1990 by the Division of Christian Education of the National Council
of Churches of Christ in the USA.*

MANUFACTURED IN THE UNITED STATES OF AMERICA

For Robert L. Wilson

Contents

Introduction: People of the Book.....................9

1. The Bible as the Church's Book.............15

2. Living in the World of the Bible............48

3. The Church as the Bible's People.......... 66

4. Formed and Ever Reformed by the Bible 82

Introduction

People of the Book

"I can't figure it out," he said to me. He was a professor at the local college, a brilliant mathematician who spent his day figuring out tough problems. So when he said that he couldn't understand something, I sat up and took notice.

"I can't figure out what makes the church different from other organizations. Our preacher is always urging us to invite someone to church with us. He says that we need new members. And I sit there, as the preacher talks, asking myself, 'Why would I invite someone to be part of this?'"

He continued, "It isn't that I'm opposed to the church. Who could be opposed to the church? I don't have anything against what we do there on a Sunday morning. It's just . . ."

"It's just what?" I asked.

"It's just that I don't see anything different or special about what we do on Sunday in church, and what's going on at any number of other very helpful organizations. Friendliness? Caring? I get all that at Rotary. And when the preacher talks, it's mostly advice. Mostly good advice, but no different from that which I might get anywhere else— advice about how to raise my kids, how to have a happy marriage, how to get along in life. At least Rotary meets at a convenient time of the week!"

His comments struck me as so basic, so threateningly to the heart of the matter, that they troubled me for some time. What would you say to him?

We could say that the church is a caring and loving community, a group of people who are deeply concerned about the welfare of the less fortunate. Any number of other helpful human organizations could make such claims. A host of other community agencies care about the youth, reach out to older people, work for justice for the poor. And it doesn't help to say that the church is somehow *more* concerned about the youth, the elderly, the poor than these other groups. That argument can as easily be turned back upon the church.

"The Durham Bulls [our local baseball team] has done more to bring black and white people together than the church ever thought about. A

Saturday evening at the Durham Bulls is more racially inclusive than a Sunday in any church in town," she said. And she was right.

So we are left with our question. What makes the church, your congregation and mine, different, utterly essential, without equal, unique? Let me venture a response: *A congregation is Christian to the degree that it is confronted by and attempts to form its life in response to the Word of God.*

As Christians, we are people of a book, the Bible. That doesn't mean we worship the Bible or that we claim to have somehow captured God between the pages of a book. It means that in our life with the Bible, we claim to have been confronted by the living Lord.

We use that phrase "Word of God" in a more dynamic sense than just referring to the words of the Bible.

John begins his Good News by announcing:

> In the beginning was the Word, and the Word was with God, and the Word was God. He was in the beginning with God. . . . In him was life, and the life was the light of all people. The light shines in the darkness, and the darkness did not overcome it. . . . And the Word became flesh and lived among us, and we have seen his glory, the glory of a father's only son, full of grace and truth.
>
> (John 1.1-2, 4-5, 14)

That "Word" was the Christ, Jesus. Jesus is God's supreme act of self-communication. Yet we would not have known to expect the Christ had we not been taught by the Hebrew scriptures to expect God to love us by speaking to us, had we not been taught to listen for the Word of God by reading the Word of God which is scripture. The nation of Israel, and later the church, are a people formed by God's speaking and our listening, a community given birth by God's communication with us through scripture.

"Long ago God spoke to our ancestors in many and various ways by the prophets; but in these last days he has spoken to us by a Son." (Hebrews 1:1-2)

That divine-human dialogue is the originating event of the church. A congregation can fail at many things and still succeed; however, if it fails to be, or at least struggles to become, a people of the Bible, then it might as well stop meeting on Sunday mornings and meet instead for lunch on Wednesdays like any other well-intentioned civic club.

A Christian and a Buddhist differ, not because one is sincere and the other is not, nor because one is necessarily a "better person" than the other. We differ because we have listened to different stories, lived our lives by different words. While there may be certain similarities among people of different religions, they will be different because their sacred writings are different, because they have attended to different accounts of the way the world is put together.

Because we have been so willing to accommodate the message of the Bible to the limitations of contemporary culture, the modern world does not regard the church as a threat; I suspect that it regards us as merely boring. We are giving the modern world less and less in which to disbelieve because it senses no difference between what the church is saying and what is being said by a variety of secular voices. Thus, the modern world is *not* called upon actively to decide for or against the church, because it sees in the church so little against which to take a stand. The world which once imprisoned our ancestors now responds to an utterly enculturated church with mere indifference.

This book is an exploration of the way your congregation is formed by its confrontation with the Bible. We will inquire into the ways that scripture *forms us, reforms us,* and *challenges us,* as well as the ways that we hide from, close our ears to, and evade the Bible's claim upon us.

Our discussion takes place with the conviction that every revival of the church, every reformation of God's people, has arisen out of a fresh hearing of scripture, a new appropriation of the demands of the text in our life together.

Many people today are concerned about the decline in the membership and influence of churches within mainline Protestantism. Their concern is justified. Yet such concerns are also dangerous to the integrity of the church if they are not guided by the conviction that the church is more than just another helpful human organization. The church is the main means whereby God speaks and we listen, whereby we are taught to speak to God with the conviction that God hears *and* cares. The supreme evidence of that divine-human dialogue is the Bible. The divinely established terms for that dialogue are asserted in the Bible, everything which we need to know is here, in order that we might have life more abundantly.

May this book be an invitation to renewal within your congregation.

WILLIAM H. WILLIMON

Duke University Chapel

Advent 1990

1

The Bible as the Church's Book

Jesus returns to his hometown synagogue in Nazareth (Luke 4:16-20). What does Israel do on its holiest of days? Luke gives us a picture of the People of God gathered.

> When he came to Nazareth, where he had been brought up, he went to the synagogue on the sabbath day, as was his custom. He stood up to read, and the scroll of the prophet Isaiah was given to him. He unrolled the scroll and found the place where it was written:
> "The Spirit of the Lord is upon me,
>   because he has anointed me
>   to bring good news to the poor.
>   He has sent me to proclaim
>   release to the captives

and recovery of sight to the blind,
   to let the oppressed go free,
 to proclaim the year of the
    Lord's favor."

And he rolled up the scroll, gave it back to the attendant, and sat down. The eyes of all in the synagogue were fixed on him. Then he began to say to them, "Today this scripture has been fulfilled in your hearing." All spoke well of him and were amazed at the gracious words that came from his mouth. They said, "Is not this Joseph's son?" He said to them, "Doubtless you will quote to me this proverb, 'Doctor, cure yourself!' And you will say, 'Do here also in your hometown the things that we have heard you did at Capernaum.'" And he said, "Truly I tell you, no prophet is accepted in the prophet's hometown. But the truth is, there were many widows in Israel in the time of Elijah, when the heaven was shut up three years and six months, and there was a severe famine over all the land; yet Elijah was sent to none of them except to a widow at Zarephath in Sidon. There were also many lepers in Israel in the time of the prophet Elisha, and none of them was cleansed except Naaman the Syrian." When they heard this, all in the synagogue were filled with rage. They got up, drove him out of the town, and led him to the brow of the hill on which their town was built, so that they might hurl him off the cliff. But he passed through the midst of them and went on his way.

Jesus returns to his hometown synagogue. And what do they do? They hand him the scroll, the scriptures of Israel. They do not ask Jesus, "Tell us how it is for you." They do not ask him to report on his days at college or to share his feelings with them. They hand him the scroll and ask him to read. *Then* he interprets, *then* he preaches. Watch closely as they hand him the scroll. In that action, we see a movement which is at the very heart of the faith of Israel.

There may be religions which begin with long walks in the woods, communing with nature, getting close to trees. There may be religions which begin by delving into the recesses of a person's ego, rummaging around in the psyche. However, Christianity is not one of those.

Christianity is a people who begin with the action of taking up the scroll and being confronted with stories of God. These stories insert themselves into our accustomed ways of doing business and challenge us to change or else be out-of-step with the way things are now that God has entered human history.

They hand Jesus the scroll. He reads from the prophet Isaiah, speaking of that day when God would again act to set things right, to come for Israel, to lift up the downtrodden and push down the mighty. The Spirit of the Lord is upon me to announce God's advent.

After reading, Jesus begins to interpret. Note that he interprets by setting other biblical stories next to Isaiah's announcement of God's advent. "God is coming among us. And the last time God came among us, during the days of the great prophet Elijah, many of our own people were hungry. But God's prophet fed none of them. Only a widow from Sidon, a foreigner, was nourished."

The congregation grows silent. The young preacher continues. "And were not there many sick people in Israel during the time of the prophet Elisha? Yes. But Elisha healed none of them. Only Naaman, a Syrian, a Syrian army officer."

And the once adoring congregation became an angry mob. As they led the young preacher out, he said to them, "I said nothing new. It's all in the book! It's all in *your* book!"

A distinctive community is being formed here by this reading and listening. A peculiar community is being criticized here as well. What sort of people are being called into being by such stories?

The Politics of the Bible

The church was called into being, as if out of nothing, as a people in dialogue with scripture. Unlike conventional means of human organization, the church had no ethnic, gender, or national basis for unity. All it had were these stories called scripture. These scriptures rendered a person, a personality, Jesus. For this new and distinctive community called the church, Jesus of Nazareth, as the Messiah, became the interpretive framework for all reality, the organizing principle for all of life. Thus the function of scripture was political, constitutive. By "political" I do not mean politics as it has degenerated in our own time—the aggressive securing of individual rights, the maximum number of personal desires elevated to the level of needs which are then pursued at all cost. The Bible is "political" in the classic sense of the word politics—the formation of a *polis*, the constitution of a people through a discussion of what needs are worth having, what goals are good.

Thus the Bible must be read "politically," that is, it must be read from the awareness of its desire to form a new people. We would not read Shakespeare's *King Lear* as history or as science. It is a drama. So we should not read the Bible as merely science, history, philology, or personal help. The Bible seeks to engender a people, a *polis*.

In defiance of sociological laws, without conventional cultural, or ethnic support, this new community conquered the Roman Empire in one of the most amazing cultural shifts ever seen in Western history. For instance, there was no value more dear to classical Romans than the family. All of Roman society was organized around the family headed by the *Pater Familias*, the father of the family. Marriage, political power, economic advancement, civil rights were all based upon the family. Family name and status determined a person's situation throughout life. Indeed, the military was virtually the only means of social advancement for someone born into a poor Roman family.

From the beginning, the church was, in complete contrast to Roman society, ambivalent or even hostile to the family. Early Christian leaders like Paul advised against marriage and familial attachments. Christian baptism had as its goal nothing less than the disruption of one's family since one was "re-born" in baptism. The prior natural birth into a human family was overcome through the new birth of baptism so that the family name was changed and one was given a new Christian name, a new identity. This identity was based upon the new standards of adoption into a new family—the church. In baptism, the old distinctions by which the world lives were washed away.

> As many of you as were baptized into Christ have clothed yourself with Christ. There is no longer Jew or Greek, there is no longer slave or free, there is no longer male and female; for all of you are one in Christ Jesus.
> (Galatians 3:27-28)

In other words, *the Bible had reality-defining power over the church*. Through scripture we were taught to view and review the world through new categories. Among Christians there could be no deference to family name, gender, race, or economic position. All of those old, dated distinctions had become washed in the waters of baptism.

Scripture gave us a new story, a new narrative account of the way the world was put together, new direction for history, new purpose for being on earth. The world of Rome had many other stories which gave meaning to peoples' lives: eroticism, pantheism, polytheism, cynicism. To be a Christian was to be someone who had been initiated, by baptism, into this alternative story of the world.

It was not the case that ancient Romans felt some inner need in their lives, some vague feeling of emptiness and then went shopping about for a faith that would fill it, found Christianity and then embraced it. Rather, it was that the church incorporated ancient Romans into their story of reality called scripture. The church gave them a different story through which to make sense out of their lives.

When you read scripture, you will note that narrative, or story, is the Bible's primary means of dealing with truth. Occasionally, but only rarely, will the Bible attempt to define the essence of something. Socrates was interested in discovering a good working definition of big words like "truth," and "beauty," but that is not the Bible's way of working. In the Bible, a Jewish carpenter's son comes forward and says, "I am the way, the truth, the life." We must follow his story if we are to know truth.

Occasionally, but only rarely, will the Bible describe some inner, personal experience. Our time is an age in which people are greatly infatuated with themselves, their own feelings, their personal stories. The longest journey most of us venture is the rather short trip deep into the recesses of our own egos. This is not the Bible's path to truth.

Rather, the Bible seeks to catch our lives up in a grand adventure, a great saga of God's dealings with humanity—a saga begun in God's journey with Israel, continued in the surprising call of God even unto the Gentiles. The church is the product of that story.

Modernity and the Bible

When the Bible is read from a viewpoint other than its attempt to engender a new family, it is misread.

Thomas Jefferson, that brilliant early member of the modern age, went through the Bible and excised all of the passages which dealt with miracles or other supernatural occurrences because Jefferson equated supernatural with "superstitious." He sought a faith of reason—the great value of the eighteenth-century European Enlightenment. Jefferson's purified Bible was considerably shorter than the original!

Jefferson was one of the first "modern" critics of the Bible, one of the earliest interpreters of scripture who attempted to make scripture conform to the needs and expectations of modern people. He thus led the way for the chief method of abusing the Bible in our age.

Theologian Thomas Oden says that accommodation is the hallmark of contemporary theology. In his book, *After Modernity . . . What*, he says, "The fundamental *eros* of the leading contemporary theological traditions of Bultmann, Tillich, Bonhoeffer, Whitehead, and Rahner is accommodation to modernity. This is the underlying motif that unites the seemingly vast differences between many forms of existential theology, process theology, liberation theology, and demythologization—all are searching for some more compatible assessment to modernity . . . the process called 'modernization' implies that a society is undergoing a change from traditional to modern values, technology, or beliefs. There is an air of hubris [pride] about the term—it invariably assumes its own superiority."

The Bible's purpose has been misrepresented through certain modern methods of reading scripture. As we have said, scripture is a story which has a "political" function, namely, to form and to critique a new community, a peculiar people, the church.

Modernity asks not, "How is the Bible shaping a new reality among us?" but rather it asks, "Does the Bible report accurately the events it is describing?" Narrative meaning, story, is lost in debates over facticity. "Facts" are defined as that which can be verified through scientific or historical research. Meaning is limited to that which can be derived through science or history. This is the equivalent to evaluating *King Lear* on the basis of how accurately it reflects the situation of the English monarchy in the Elizabethan Age or on the basis of psychotherapeutic depiction of mental illness.

Two warring camps of biblical interpreters are, in a curious way, two sides of this same coin:

Fundamentalists or inerrantists, assert that the Bible is "true" in that it is full of facts about the way the world was created, the miraculous curing of illnesses, and so forth. Fundamentalists go to great pains to demonstrate "scientifically" that Genesis is scientifically accurate. Even as I write, a biblical scholar is being fired at a seminary because he says that he has doubts that an axehead really floated on water. The narrative significance of scripture is thus lost in debates over historical or scientific "facts."

Historical critics would seem to be the polar opposite of the fundamentalists. Historical criticism began in the nineteenth century as an attempt to apply modern, scientific methods to the interpretation of scripture. The fundamentalists assert in great credulity that, if the Bible said something happened, it "really happened"; the historical critic begins with great skepticism that an event "ever happened" unless that event can be verified by some means other than the Bible itself.

Charles Hodge, in his *Systematic Theology*, was one of those who helped give birth to modern fundamentalism. Hodge wrote, "If natural science be concerned with the facts and laws of nature, theology is concerned with the facts and principles of the Bible. If the object of the one would be to arrange and systematize the facts of the external world, and to ascertain the laws by which they are determined; the object of the other is to systematize the facts of the Bible, the ascertaining of principles or general truths which those facts involve" (page 112). Common sense, when confronted with the "facts" of scripture, could rightly interpret scripture. This was a very modern reading of the Bible. It was also a very individualist and subjective reading; one which claimed that "common sense" and "facts" could be put together in such a way that one did not need a community to help interpret scripture.

Both fundamentalism and historical criticism believe that "facts," defined by the prevailing empirical methods of the modern age, are what make any document important. In an odd way, fundamentalists do not defend the Bible against the assaults of science; they capitulate to science, making science the supreme validator of scripture. The goal of both is the great goal of an insecure modern age—the security and certainty of absolute objectivity.

In the hands of both the fundamentalists and the historical critics, the Bible becomes fragmented, uninteresting. The story and its political claim upon us is lost in debates over "what really happened." Modern infatuations—historicism, science, life based only upon what I can know and prove through empirical means—are applied to the Bible in ways that have little to do with the Bible's original intent. Facts, even miraculous ones, tend not to be self-involving. The significance of the Bible is sought somewhere other than in the Bible or in the community it claims to be producing. So nineteenth-century German pietists claimed that the Bible was valuable because it so well described general human experience. Eighteenth-century rationalists like Thomas Jefferson found in the Bible a repository of great, general truth. Kant claimed that the Bible, even though quite unreliable from the standpoint of history or science, was still a valuable source of moral thought.

Some other worthy human value—morality, reason, history, science, emotion—sat as judge and jury on the value of the Bible. Both fundamentalists and historical critics assumed that it is possible for the Bible to make sense apart from the living, breathing community which makes it make sense. Both groups assumed that it was possible to understand the Bible, the church's book, without being converted into the church's faith.

The roots of this strange reading of the Bible stem out of two seventeenth-century sources:

Science was given birth in the seventeenth century. Through scientifically derived facts,

26

humanity could lift itself out of the mire of mere human opinion. Amidst conflicting truth claims and superstition, the scientific method delivered incorrigibly self-evident truth, or so it was assumed.

The Wars of Religion were another factor which contributed to a shift in our reading of scripture. Europe found itself, in the seventeenth century, exhausted and bloodied by seemingly endless "wars of religion." The causes for the turmoil were as much political as religious; that is, religion was the "glue" which held nations together during the Middle Ages. When that cohesion was threatened by shifts in religious outlook, nations were destabilized and the result was politically chaotic. Religion, which nations had relied upon for political stability since the Holy Roman Empire, became a political liability rather than an asset. The threat of anarchy led to a flight away from the authority of churches and their hierarchies toward *individual conscience and reason.* Each individual now had the right to decide on the Bible, to interpret scripture.

The new, emerging nation-state found individuals easier to manage than institutions and groups. Detached, isolated individuals appear to be more malleable than people who must answer to some higher authority other than themselves. In a curious sense, the notion of the autonomous, sovereign individual is a corollary of the sovereign nation state. The state became the new organizing principle for human life, the main protector of life

27

from the cradle to the grave, the chief source of meaning and identity for modern people. Today, when occasionally someone asserts that religion is the chief cause of strife in the world—when Hindus battle Moslems in the East, or Catholics fight Protestants in Northern Ireland—what they usually mean is that if all these religious people would only convert their religious loyalties into nationalistic ones we would have peace. In other words, limit the claim of our religion to the claims of the almighty state as the rest of us modern people have done.

One of the goals of the Enlightenment and the liberal democracies that it created was to rise above the bloody religious conflict of the seventeenth century. By subordinating beliefs about God, religious identities, and the claims of religious communities to the claims of the new modern nation, enlightened philosophers hoped for a world in which people would no longer kill one another in the name of God. The irony is that since the triumph of the Enlightenment, people no longer kill one another in the name of God. Now we kill on a scale unknown in the seventeenth century, in the name of the new nation-state. We have created a world in which people are convinced that it is wrong to kill, unless the nation is threatened because the nation now provides people with a source of ultimate identity, protection, and meaning in life. It is the nation which gives us our "freedom" to be individuals. And since our individual freedom means everything,

28

the nation, as the alleged source of individual freedom, becomes our supreme value.

Of course, as Christians, we have no stake in wanting a world in which people kill in the name of God. (There are religions which encourage people from time to time to kill in God's name. Christianity is not one of those.) However, we should note that we have "progressed" to a point where people now believe it outrageous to kill for religion, but quite natural to kill for the state. It is ironic that in its attempt to overcome the imperialism of religion, the Enlightenment submitted us to the most bloody imperialism in all of human history—the modern state. In fact, when one counts all of the people who have been killed in this century *by their own governments*, one must conclude the modern nation to be the most disastrous of all human inventions.

People were told that violence could be avoided if we would use our "reason." Often the Bible was contrasted with reason. The Bible was an old, pre-modern, therefore pre-reasonable collection of superstition, opinion, a few facts and much error. One of the things which the advocates of this "reason" failed to grasp was that their notion of reason was itself dependent upon a story, dependent upon a narrative account of the world. There is no such thing as independent, individually-possessed reason. Reason is not some innate human talent with which we are born. Most modern people think of reason as an innate capacity which can be freely exercised if we simply strip ourselves of all communally-derived traditions, prejudices, and emotions. This is an eighteenth-century fiction which has no basis in reality. The very notion of reason as independent, individual, innate, is itself dependent upon an eighteenth-century account of human nature and the world. A Hindu who did not share this story of the reasonable, solitary individual would have no idea what the word "reason" means. If we were to say to this person from India, "Be reasonable now," what would she think?

The notion that our eighteenth-century-created "reason" was a universal human attribute, the very hallmark of our basic humanity, had a darker side. If people were found to be basically "unreasonable"—as we defined reason—then there could be only one explanation for them. They must be sub-human. So eighteenth-century Europeans felt justified in enslaving Africa because its people seemed to lack those attributes which made human beings human—individuality, autonomy, reason. So nineteenth-century Americans had few misgivings about exterminating and uprooting millions of Native Americans because, with their tribalism, primitive cultures, and premodern ways, these people were obviously "savages," and we modern, nationalistic, "reasonable" people were right to overcome them, as "reason" was destined to overcome superstition. In the twentieth century, the Nazis charged that Jews in Europe were

"tribal," disloyal to the modern nation, superstitious, and irrational.

Ironically, the rise of the autonomous individual,
individually applying "reason" to the questions of
life, which was to produce a world free of the violent
religious conflict which Europe had known in the
seventeenth century, gave us the intellectual
equipment we needed to make the twentieth
century the bloodiest of all. When we dropped the
bomb on civilians in Japan, Americans were told
that the Japanese were "irrational," that they did
not value human life as much as we, and that they
were maniacal fanatics. Our "reason" was revealed
to be a decidedly two-edged sword, a path to as
much inhumanity as humanity.

Our much praised "reason" was but a culturally
conditioned, limited, yet often useful, way of
looking at the world. The notion of reason had
been helpful in forming modern European society,
in setting up constitutional democracies, in giving
birth to science. But it definitely had its more
sinister side, particularly when it was used against
those people and cultures who did not appear to fit
our definitions of what it meant to be "rational"
and therefore "human."

It is not that the Bible is unreasonable whereas
modern, secular, scientific people now have
reason. It is that the Bible has a very different
definition of what it means to think, to be
reasonable. In most of the New Testament, we
become "reasonable"—truthful, honest, accurate,

coherent—only after we are converted into the truth which is Jesus Christ. Reason is not some detached, individual endowment. Reason is a result of conversion *into*, and life *within* a distinctive community which has been given the skills, through this story called scripture, for seeing the world and our lives rightly.

Fundamentalism is a peculiarly modernist approach to biblical interpretation. It has its roots in Scottish common sense philosophy which teaches that the only means of convincing anyone of anything is through common sense, by elucidating those facts in life which are so apparent, so self-evident, that the facts convince someone by mere common sense. Fundamentalism believes that there are certain self-evident facts within scripture which are so obviously true, so apparently factual, that one need only uncover them, assert them, and people will be compelled to affirm them on the basis of everyday common sense.

Both fundamentalism and higher criticism wish to make the truth of Christianity available to all without training, without the disciplines of a community, assuming that all one needs to appropriate the meaning of a biblical text is to get clear about the "facts" of the text.

But "facts" tend not to be as "factual" as we like to think. (For a wonderful discussion of the questionable modern split between "fact" and "value" see Lesslie Newbigin, *Foolishness to the Greeks: The Gospel and Western Culture* [Grand Rapids: Eerdmans, 1986], pp. 74-80.) We assume that whereas values are dependent upon a context, a point of view of the person who holds those values, facts are not dependent on a context. A fact is a fact to a person in Calcutta, Calgary, or Cairo. One of the great lures of scientific "facts" is that they appear to be self-evident to anyone, Hindu or Christian, as facts. If only we could uncover such facts in the Bible! But even our supposedly self-evident "facts" are often more context dependent, story dependent than we know.

The Limits of Historical Criticism of Scripture

Modern historical criticism hoped to dig beneath the accumulated historical deposits of the Bible and uncover the facts. Historical criticism positively contributed to the church's confrontation with the Bible. We were reminded, by the tools of historical study, that the Bible is a culturally, historically-conditioned product. We were shown the great gap which stands between our time and the time of the Bible. Words take on different meanings over the years. Contexts change. For instance, after Martin Luther's great discovery and subsequent stress upon justification by faith—the doctrine that we are saved, not by our human good works, but by God's gracious justification of us in Christ —Protestant biblical interpretation tended to find justification by faith on every page of the New Testament. It was said that Paul became disillusioned with Judaism because he discovered how futile it was to obey the burden of the Law. Then he found justification by faith.

But historical criticism, in its studies of Pauline texts, in its research into the notion of the Law in Judaism, revealed to us how we had imposed Luther's reading of Paul upon the historical Paul. The main revelation to Paul was not that the Law was evil but that Jesus was the Messiah. Paul argued that Jesus was the fulfillment of the promises of Israel, not their negation. Historical criticism helped to correct our externally imposed reading of the Bible.

Yet there were losses. Modern biblical scholarship tended to teach us what texts *did not* mean in the past, rather than what they meant today. The available critical tools such as historical research, philological research (word study), and textual reconstruction—tended to determine what was significant in the biblical text.

I was taught in seminary that the first question to ask of a text is, "What did this passage originally mean?" Who decided that a definition of historical meaning was the primary question to ask of the Bible? For one thing, such a question implies that we have the tools to answer the question—which may be a very questionable assumption. It is very, very difficult to go back two thousand years or more, peel away accumulated layers of a text, and make some guess about the historical circumstances of a passage when the passage says virtually nothing about its historical setting.

Historical criticism has difficulty delivering on its promise: to put a given biblical text into its historic context and then to apply that same meaning to the church today. Why should we begin asking the questionable, "What did this text mean?" Why not begin with something like, "What is this text saying to the church attempting to be faithful today?"

There is a rabbinic parable told about the time Moses returned from the dead and appeared at the distinguished Jewish Theological Seminary in New York. He slipped into the back of the classroom and was amazed to hear the professor lecturing rabbinical students on the meaning of the Pentateuch. (Tradition has it that Moses wrote those first five books of the Hebrew Bible.) Moses listened and became increasingly agitated with the professor's interpretation of his work. Finally, when he could stand it no longer, Moses blurted out, "This is ridiculous! You have it all wrong. I didn't mean *any* of that when I wrote the Pentateuch."

The parable ends with the question, "Who is right, the professor or Moses?"

We have been conditioned to think that Moses was right. After all, so the argument goes, Moses was the author. The meaning of the words in Moses' mind are the most important data about the text. The correct answer, from the Rabbinic point of view, is that Moses was wrong. The Bible is not a dead document, some ancient deposit that we are to protect and to mine occasionally. A living church has a living relationship with the Bible. Scripture must be interpreted with tradition. It is quite natural that in each new age, the church should find new meaning in scripture, new challenges, new significance in the text which has not been evident before. Nowhere does the Bible lay claim to self-sufficiency. It is the church's book.

Both fundamentalism and historical criticism tend to shackle the Bible with abstract, external standards of alleged objectivity. The goal of these two methods of interpretation is to free the individual consciousness from the demands of the church and the community-forming power of scripture. By declaring scripture somehow self-sufficient, and somehow making sense apart from the community that makes it make sense, we have only exposed scripture to subjective, arbitrary interpretation.

Consider this analogy of the intellectual limits of the historical critical method of interpreting the Bible: A letter is found in an attic of an old, abandoned house. The letter is not dated or postmarked. All that can be said for sure is that it seems to be in a woman's handwriting and it is addressed to someone named John. What can we tell about the letter? The letter begins:

Dear John, I write this to you as I gaze upon these red roses. I think of you. You have been through some terribly difficult days but now you must pull yourself together and have hope. While there has been much confusion and difficulty for you in the past couple of years, I am certain that the future will be better for you. You must forget what is past, old hurts and fears, past trials, and look forward to tomorrow. Love, Jane.

A biblical critic examines the letter and speculates that the woman who wrote the letter was an aristocratic person. Why? She mentions the "red roses." Only a rich person could afford to be writing a letter in a rose garden. The "terribly difficult days" are possibly days of war. It has been a time of national disaster. She is attempting to comfort her lover who has been through a great trial, possibly a battle. She wants to give him hope and comfort for tomorrow.

Eventually, it is discovered that the letter was written by Jane Smith, aunt of John Smith. She wrote it to John, not during a war, but in 1965 when John had just been jilted by his girlfriend whom he had hoped to marry. Aunt Jane wrote to John, not from a rose garden but from a cheap motel room in Cleveland where the walls were covered in some dated, horrible wallpaper imprinted with red roses.

See? For all of our sincere historical speculation, we learned very little of lasting value, certainly very little useful information from our historical digging.

What *can* we learn? Well, about the only thing we thought about this letter that proved to be true was *the basic intent* of the letter, the basic thrust of its purpose. It was written by someone attempting to encourage another person in a time of need. The writer did so, not on the basis of some appeal to God, or good luck, but rather on the basis of her assurance that somehow, some way, "the future will be better for you."

Thus we are really limited, in our confrontation with the Bible, if the main thing we want to know is, "What did this originally mean?" History cannot tell us all that we might like to know to answer that question. But is that question the primary question to ask? As we have noted in the little analogy above, even though it is tough to discern the originating date, identity of the writer or the audience, and precise historical setting, by reading the text itself we can discern probable intent. What was this text attempting to do for the church? Encourage? Judge? Inform? Correct? Convert?

And that may be quite enough to make scripture very interesting for today's church. If one approaches scripture only as one would approach a book on ancient history, or as a collection of ancient Near Eastern literature, then that does not sound too interesting. Let's be honest. There are better sources of history and there is better literature to be had elsewhere. However, if scripture is approached for its "political" value, that is, for its ability to engender and to critique the synagogue and church, then we already have the needed tools to engage scripture today.

In the past century, theologians and biblical interpreters have made a great deal out of modernity. They present themselves as intellectual evangelists who desperately want to cast the word of the gospel into terms that will be intelligible to "the modern mind." Modern people can no longer believe in the miracles and special divine revelation, hence biblical faith must be "demythologized" to meet the intellectual challenges of a completely new era. Modern people were said to be secular, people no longer shaped by the institutions of Christianity, people who had to be appealed to through their sense of individualism and autonomy.

The primary strategy adopted by many biblical interpreters and theologians was to baptize the values of the secular person as being more Christian than those of the traditional believer (Tillich) and then to join the secular person in whatever his or her quest might be. If the modern person claimed to be deeply concerned about justice, then justice was presented as the Bible's agenda. If the modern person seemed to be primarily interested in self-fulfillment, then that quest was lifted up as central to the Bible.

Today, when the self-confident, exaggerated claims of modernity are being severely questioned, biblical interpreters and churches which have married the spirit of the age are bereft of direction. Obviously, my contention is that we should not take modernity too seriously—or that we should at least take it on *our* terms rather than *its* terms. The modern world has taught us to approach biblical texts with suspicion. I am suggesting that we approach them out of a kind of naivete. Part of that naivete is born out of an awareness of the limitations of our point of view. We are usually able to see the Bible's cultural limitations more easily than our own. Having some sense of our own cultural limitations, the limits of modernity, enables us to approach the Bible with a more belief-full naivete. That is, modernity is simply one in a long line of ideological competitors to challenge the Christian faith.

Our faith began from a conviction of the truthfulness of Christian claims, the superiority of the Christian vision, a superiority which we have no other way of demonstrating other than by our life together in the community which is formed by these claims. Your congregation and mine are the test for the truthfulness of the Bible. The claims of the Bible rise or fall, not on the basis of their alleged universality ("Everyone believes this, even if they do not believe in Jesus.") or their applicability in helping us with our various individual goals ("The Bible can help you to be a success in the business of living.") The claims of the Bible are vindicated only when we can point to living, breathing congregations whose life together embodies the Bible.

One Sunday I was preaching on Luke 16:19-31, the story of "Lazarus and the Rich Man." In my sermon, I noted how most of us are in the position of the Rich Man, that is, most of us have had all that we needed in life. Our children have never gone hungry, we have not lived in utter poverty, we have always had enough. We have received our reward. However, that is not true for most of the people of the world.

Then as part of the sermon, I simply read a clipping from a newspaper which told about the practice in Brazil of poor people selling organs of their bodies to rich buyers. The news story told about how there is a brisk business in human organs. The newspaper also told about a man named Walter who had sold both of his eyes for $20,000. Walter had two children and had never held a regular job in his entire life. He was quoted as saying, "Now I can see that my family has a better life." The better life which Walter wanted to "see" for his family was bought at the expense of both of his eyes.

Then I simply ended the sermon, we had a few prayers, a hymn, and we all went home for lunch.

The next morning, when I arrived at my office, the telephone was ringing. It was Debbie. "I hardly slept at all last night," she began.

"I could not get that poor man out of my mind. I kept thinking about Walter."

Debbie and her husband lived in a very modest house, in a very modest part of town. He was a young professor at a nearby college. "I woke up my husband early this morning and told him that we were going to have to examine our life-style. We were going to buy a new car, but we really don't need a new one. We can get our old one fixed. We were going to buy a new stereo. We certainly can get along without that. The reason I am calling you is to tell you that we want to double our giving to the church if you can assure us that some of it has a good chance of reaching someone like Walter."

I had to confess that I had slept well that evening, after delivering that sermon. However, Debbie had heard the sermon. The biblical story had penetrated her life in such a way that her life was changed. If the biblical story is incapable of producing a church which is able to produce someone like Debbie, then no amount of intellectual gymnastics can make the Bible credible. The best proof of the Bible, the best proof of the resurrection and the claims of faith, are changed lives who embody the Bible's beliefs.

In your church and mine, we approach scripture with the conviction that the Bible wants to do (intention) to today's church what the Bible wanted to do to yesterday's church. The Bible is busy forming a new people, engendering a covenant community, a people who are encountered by a living Lord who meets us in scripture and thereby changes us.

We need never be surprised that, when we read the Bible, we encounter a collision between our current way of thinking and the Bible's way of thinking. The Bible strives, not just for agreement, but for radical conversion. Any way of reading the Bible which by-passes the possibility of conversion, is not reading the Bible on the basis of its own claims. Biblical scholar, Walter Wink, in criticizing historical biblical criticism, has said that the biblical critic was "Not nearly so interested in being changed by the reading of the Bible, as in changing the way that the Bible was read in order to conform to the modern spirit."

If the Bible is incapable of forming new people, or if we are unwilling to be formed and reformed by the Bible, then I can think of little need to read it. Personally, I find it rather perplexing (forgive me, professors in departments of religion) that someone should give his or her entire scholarly life to studying these 66 ancient books purely as ancient history or as ancient literature. There is better ancient history and better ancient literature elsewhere. In the church we study these 66 books, spend our whole lives coming back to them again and again, pondering them, singing them, repeating them (How many sermons have you heard on the Good Samaritan?) because we believe that they are the very words of life. The thing that makes them initially interesting, ultimately interesting is that generations have lived and (even more interesting) died by these 66 little books called the Bible. They are interesting only as a claim about what is true.

When the church calls the Bible "scripture" it is asserting something about the Bible's claim upon the church. These writings are not simply a conglomeration of ancient texts which just lie there awaiting to be picked apart by modern methods of historical or scientific investigation. They are scripture, the ultimate authority for our life together, the source of our identity and our vocation as the church. That is why I feel that one of the most significant things a preacher can do is to preach from the new Common Lectionary. The lectionary is a time-honored, ecumenical practice of using a selected table of lessons for reading in the church on Sundays. Every Sunday there is an appointed Psalm, Old Testament, Epistle, and Gospel lesson. The main justification for using the lectionary is that God's people ought to be exposed to a systematic reading of the Bible in church. Many preachers have found the lectionary to be a very helpful way of systematically preaching through scripture.

When the preacher makes clear that his or her text has come from that Sunday's appointed lectionary readings the preacher is thus signifying that he or she preaches, not merely from personal opinion, not merely to vent pet peeves, but that we preach what the church expects to be preached. These texts have a claim upon the church. We are answerable to this scripture. The Bible stands above and beyond the preacher's own concerns and limitations, sometimes standing with the congregation and its struggles, sometimes standing against us, but always there as our scripture.

One Sunday my associate pastor led the Prayer

for Others during our worship service. As part of her prayer, she prayed for "the people of Iraq, as well as all people who live in conditions of war or the threat of war."

At the end of the service, I was accosted by a very angry person who told me that she was "offended by the prayer."

When I asked her what offended her, she said, "Don't you realize that we must stand behind our troops in Saudi Arabia? How dare you lift up, in such a positive way, the people who are our sworn enemies?"

It seemed that what we had here was a clash of biblical affirmation with conventional American wisdom. In our world, of course, we must not give aid or comfort to our enemies. But in worship, in the Sunday service, we had participated in a very different world. That world was characterized, not by our usual national boundaries, the demonization of our enemies, and patriotic fervor. The world of the Bible is characterized by such outrageous passages as, "You have heard that it was said, 'you shall love your neighbor and hate your enemy.' But I say to you, Love your enemies and pray for those who persecute you, so that you may be the children of your Father who is in heaven; for he makes his sun to rise on the evil and on the good, and sends his rain on the just and the unjust " (Matt. 5:43-45).

Praying for our enemies has nothing to do with the fantasy that our enemies should just be nice people, after all. Praying for enemies is not a strategy to get ahead in the world by being nice. It has to do with responding to the world by the way that the Bible teaches. It has to do with evocation of a world which we would not have known without the testimony of the Bible. A world is evoked where enemies are prayed for rather than cursed, and we come to see ourselves as united by a God who manages to send sun upon the evil and the good, and rain upon the just and the unjust. We can pray for our enemies because, unlike the rest of the world, we know a story about a Savior who came and preached to a congregation in Nazareth, reminding them that, when the prophets of God came to save God's people, they also went to those whom God's people regarded as enemies and outsiders (Luke 4:20-28).

So, when I preach from the lectionary and I have done particularly well as a biblical preacher, and someone meets me at the door after the service saying something like, "That was the strangest thing I ever heard," I do not take offense. After all, I was not preaching *my* scripture. I was preaching the church's scripture, their scripture. I am not the one who has called this people together. God has called them forth to listen, not to me, but to scripture. I like the way in which the lectionary makes that visible and explicit.

Unfortunately much contemporary biblical criticism reads the Bible in the abstract, detached from the community. I agree with Walter Wink's opinion (*The Bible in Human Transformation*) that biblical criticism "sought to free itself from the community in order to pursue its work untrammelled," and in the process has become "cut off from any community for whose life its results might be significant . . . The community of reference and accountability became, not the liberal church but the guild of biblical scholars" who had a vested professional interest in building the influence of the university and perpetuating their methods, in enforcing conformity to their professional peer-group values rather than building up the congregation.

In fact, one suspects that certain modern ways of reading the Bible—like fundamentalism and historical criticism—arose because we no longer had a church to read the Bible. That is, in the modern age we no longer had a community of faith which understood itself to be under the claim of scripture. What we had were a conglomerate of isolated individuals, each coming to the Bible for individual reasons, with individual questions, expecting to receive individual direction. As we have noted, this is a peculiar, unnatural usage of the Bible, one for which it was never intended. In your church and mine, when God's people gather, when the Bible is opened, read, and interpreted (just as Jesus did so that day in Nazareth), the Bible is thriving in its native habitat; the political, community-forming ability of the Bible becomes apparent, and we are able to say "Amen" to Jesus' claim: "This day this scripture has been fulfilled in your hearing."

2

Living in the World of the Bible

"About that time Herod the king laid violent hands upon some who belonged to the church. He had James, the brother of John, killed with the sword; . . . he proceeded to arrest Peter also." (Acts 12:1-3)

That's what kings do. With a wave of the hand or a stroke of the pen they are able to put the forces in motion whereby "violent hands" are laid upon little people who have no power. Peter is now in jail. Where is the church?

"While Peter was kept in prison, the church prayed fervently to God for him." (12:5) There is Peter in jail, securely bound in chains, guarded by no less than four squads of soldiers, and there is the church, praying for Peter's release.

"Oh Lord, please do something for Peter," they must have prayed.

The very night before Herod was going to bring him out [to kill him as he killed James?], Peter, bound with two chains, was sleeping between two soldiers while guards in front of the door were keeping watch over the prison. [Note the great detail in describing how securely Peter was being guarded. Obviously no one could escape from such a prison!] Suddenly an angel of the Lord appeared and a light shone in the cell. He tapped Peter on the side and woke him, saying, "Get up quickly." (12:6-7)

Note that Peter (earlier named "The Rock" by Jesus, the rock of the church, our leader) must be struck on the side in order to be awakened. Peter was apparently the last person in the world to expect liberation from this Roman jail. He had accepted his fate, resigned himself to his situation. After all, as we say, "You can't fight City Hall." What can just one little person do when up against so mighty a power as Imperial Rome? Better just to go to sleep.

The angel leads the half-dazed Peter through one door after another out toward the street, out toward freedom. "Then Peter came to himself and said, 'Now I am sure that the Lord has sent his angel and rescued me from the hands of Herod and from all that the . . . people were expecting.'" (12:11)

Now Peter returns to the church, to "the house of Mary, the mother of John . . . where many had gathered and were praying." (12:12) Notice something unusual about this church? It is meeting at a woman's house. A *woman's* house. That would not have been done in polite, conventional society. Obviously, this new people, this church is an unusual group of people. Here they are, meeting in a woman's house, being led by women.

So they are at Mary's house praying for Peter's release. Their prayer is interrupted by a wonderfully comic scene in which a maid, Rhoda answers the knock at the door, hurries back in excitement to tell the church that Peter is loose, standing at the door, knocking. "They said to her, 'You are out of your mind!' But she insisted that it was so." (12:15)

Does this episode with Rhoda remind you of another story in the Bible in which women testified that someone was loose? At Easter it was women who first saw the empty tomb. But when these women ran back to Jerusalem to tell the news, the disciples (church) reacted in a similar way to how they reacted to Rhoda's testimony: "These words seemed to them an idle tale, and they did not believe them." (Luke 24:11)

Isn't it curious that the church, the very people praying for deliverance, pleading for God to act, are often the most surprised and the most incredulous when God finally acts? Luke means for us to read Acts 12 as an Easter story. He wants to make the point that Easter is not a one-time event. Easter keeps on happening. Just as the power of God defeated the powers of Caesar and raised Jesus up, setting him loose on Easter, so

God continues to defeat Caesar and set Jesus' people free at the prison. The church consists of those people who hear the Easter proclamation, doubt it at first, then are moved to belief.

Back to the story. Peter keeps on knocking frantically, after all, the soldiers could have caught up with him by now. At last the door is opened and the church was "amazed."

Now I ask you: What sort of people told this story? Who would have been given hope through the telling of such a tale? What sort of people formed themselves around this narrative?

John Calvin had spoken of scripture as the lens through which Christians view all reality. A lens brings certain things into focus and eliminates other things from our view. I could not read the words on this page without the lenses in the glasses I am now wearing. In viewing the world through the Bible, my world is taken up into scripture and thereby transformed. My world— where the poor are treated as failures, the powerful are praised as saviors, where nations are worshiped as gods—is taken up, is translated into the world of the Bible. In this translation, things take on new meanings, different significations. The people at the top like King Herod are brought low and the people whom the world places at the bottom like Rhoda are lifted up.

Now, in much of the church, the direction of biblical interpretation appears to be in reverse. Rather than finding ourselves translated into the world of the Bible, the Bible has been placed in the dock, on trial, and the biblical message is said to be irrelevant if it cannot be translated into the contemporary world view. Of course, to communicate the Bible, scripture has always been translated into contemporary idiom to some degree. But now this is being done systematically, deliberately. We begin with Marxist categories of class struggle, liberation, and economic determinism, lay this lens over the Bible, and preach only what Marxist interpretation enables us to see. Or we begin with feminism or with capitalism. The contemporary interpretation of scripture soon replaces scripture rather than leads one to it.

This is not to deny that the church's reading of scripture can be aided by reading the Bible from some explicit ideological point of view. For instance, feminism has highlighted the ways in which the Bible, and our biblical interpretation, has been conditioned and qualified by male dominated thought patterns. A generation ago, few Protestants had much good to say about Mary, the mother of Jesus. Mary was thought to be the infatuation of Roman Catholics, not the concern of Bible-believing Protestants. Contemporary feminist interpretation helped to recover Mary, to reveal the central place that she plays in a couple of the Gospels. There was no way for us to justify what we had allowed to happen to Mary, the first disciple, the first to say Yes to God's incursions at the nativity of Jesus.

But the more the Bible is translated, the more that Bible passages are voted up or down on the basis of the standards of some alien ideology, that ideology can be said to have captured the Bible.

Fortunately, most contemporary theological movements and much of the work of a century of historical criticism have had little impact upon the life of individual congregations. Often this lack of impact is attributed to cowardly preachers who are too frightened to share what they learned about the Bible from their seminary professors with the people in the pew, or to congregations who are so backward that they fail to keep up with the latest trends in modern theology. In reality, it means that most congregations have found the efforts of contemporary biblical scholarship and modern theology to be unhelpful in the tough task of embodying the faith in our time and place. Too many academic theologians write and talk to one another rather than to the church. Their standards are the latest trends in *academia* rather than the community forming task of *ecclesia*.

The Demise of Modernity

In the last chapter we noted what modernity did to scripture. Now we take time to note what has happened to modernity. The old confidence in the "modern world" as the supreme measure of all things is crumbling. In fact, many claim that you and I now live in a distinctly "post-modern" world. The European Enlightenment's great confidence in the power of detached, unaided, individual reason has been chastened in recent years by a new awareness that we human beings are socially, culturally, and narratively constructed. That is, we live our lives, we move, and think, and have our being out of a complex of stories, ideas, and habits. We have been enculturated into certain ways of viewing and living in the world. Nothing is exempt from this cultural conditioning, even the sciences.

For instance, take a moment, put down this book, and go outside and look at the position of the sun (if you are reading this book at night or on a park bench, adjust for conditions). Tell me what is going on.

You will tell me that the earth is busy moving around the sun. No one will challenge you when you say that the earth is moving around the sun. You know that; you believe that. And yet you have absolutely no "proof" for your belief that the earth travels around the sun. Any unbiased, objective observer, looking at the daily movement of the sun would see that the sun clearly revolves around the earth. It "comes up" in the east; it "goes down" in the west.

It is therefore nothing short of amazing that you are able to look upon this phenomenon and, contrary to everything that your senses tell you, say that "the earth is revolving around the sun."

An amazing "conversion" has taken place in your life, a conversion so profound and thorough that you are able to affirm that the sun is in the center of the universe despite all evidence to the contrary.

That "conversion" was worked in you through science, through the modern world view. It's enough to make a person ask how many such conversions have we gone through.

In Acts 12, when the church heard of Peter's release from prison, it could not conceive of such reality; it had no means of seeing what was happening before its eyes. Those first-century people had been subjected to a world view which could envision no greater power on earth than the power of Caesar.

Yet in listening to the story of Peter's release from that Roman jail, later generations of Christians were given the "lens" to see the world in new ways. Through this story, we were being enculturated into a different world view, a world view in which those whom we once regarded as so omnipotent don't seem so powerful after all, and those whom we once looked upon as impotent appear as victors.

That's what these Bible stories do to people.

Of course, from all that we now know, the earth really does move around the sun. I am not disputing that. However, I am noting how science and its claims are undergirded by an elaborate mythology, an ideology which teaches us to believe certain claims despite empirical evidence. It is not that science is presenting us with "objective," "unbiased" facts while religion is presenting us with subjective, biased opinions. It is that the scientific world view, the scientific method has its own set of beliefs out of which the claims and observations of science arise. We have been conditioned, enculturated to trust Copernicus rather than Genesis (or our own senses!) for our cosmology. That may be a relatively unimportant matter. Yet the question remains: How many conversions have been wrought in us?

Someone had to teach us to regard a story like Peter's imprisonment and release in Acts 12 as "fiction," or "myth," "just a Bible story."

Another analogy concerning the ways we are discovering the limits of science and the modern world view:

A concert pianist is playing a piano. You say to a scientist, "Explain that to me."

The scientist says, "A series of complex neurological events is taking place. The brain is sending commands through the nervous system to the pianist's hands making her fingers touch the keys. The keys are mechanically connected to the hammers within the piano which make various sounds. That explains what is happening."

You will note that the scientist's view of "what is happening" does not tell us a great deal about playing the piano. A wonderful human mystery has been reduced to a rather silly account of various biological, chemical, mechanical reactions.

And yet you and I live in a world which has

increasingly contented itself with such limited data. How many marvelous mysteries are we missing within our world simply because we lack the adequate language to describe them? How many questions have we stopped asking simply because we no longer possess an adequate means of response?

Modernity—which has taught us all to be so suspicious of the claims of religion—is due for a critique of its own claims. Within modernity and all that it takes for granted, and all that it refuses to discuss, is a well-developed (though usually unconscious) set of beliefs.

The "Modern Mind" of Western, secular culture, while inherently suspicious of all belief systems other than its own, is viciously protective of its own dogmas. I am indebted to George R. Hunsberger for his list of attributes of modernity. Among the unquestioningly affirmed beliefs of modernity, beliefs which can be in particular opposition to biblical people, are:

1. Only scientific or factual knowledge is *real* knowledge.

2. Statements of belief, other than those which claim to be based upon scientific facts, are mere opinions, not to be trusted.

3. All beliefs, being opinions, are equally valid (because they are equally unverifiable); but if they are *religious* beliefs, they should remain personal and private.

4. The goal of life is acquisition of material possessions.

5. Personal happiness, good health, and complete freedom from pain are reasonable expectations.

6. The capacity of human beings to know everything and to have control over everything in their lives is infinite.

7. The present life is the only life there is.

8. Sin is a fiction designed to make people feel guilty or to limit their freedom.

9. God is a personal opinion held by some people.

So it is not as if when the Bible is encountered in your congregation, that the Bible's word arises from a world of beliefs, values, and faith claims, whereas the culture to which it speaks is a neutral, valueless world of "facts." It is as if we stand at the collision of two cultures, on a battleground of two great faiths: the secular "faith" of modernity, and the theocentric faith of the Bible.

The sooner the contemporary Christian congregation understands itself as the center of two competing systems of belief, the better for the future of the Bible in the church.

The modern world would like to find some context-free criteria for adjudicating the disputes which arise from time to time between conflicting faiths. When a conflict arises, say between Christians and Muslims, modernity has asked each group to suppress its particular faith claims and be "reasonable" and "modern." What modernity does not seem willing to admit, is that its own appeal to be "reasonable" and "modern" arise out of faith claims of modernity. There are no context-free criteria for determining right and wrong. Every claim about the truth, including those claims of science and reason, arise out of a story, out of an account of the way the world is put together, out of some basic claims about the world which sound very much like religious claims.

For instance, there has recently been a much discussed case in Massachusetts where a couple, in adherence to the teachings of Christian Science, is being charged with child abuse in the death of their young son. The son died from complications arising from an untreated intestinal obstruction. Their case provides an interesting study of the clash between the modern world view and the claims of a religious movement.

Of course, the couple claims that their child was not left untreated. They "treated" him through prayer and the application of the principles of Christian Science. The child died and the medical community was outraged because this child was denied medical treatment.

However, the couple explained that they loved their child so much that they wanted him to be the beneficiary of the principles of Christian Science. Even though they knew that they were running a risk in not allowing the doctors to treat their son, they believed that the risks of involving their son within our current medical system were even greater. They made this assessment based upon their principles of faith. To the medical community, these parents appear to be cruel at worst, stupid at best.

However, in our condemnation of this couple we reveal our own great faith in the medical care system we have constructed—despite its grave limitations. While I am not defending the actions of the Christian Science parents, indeed I heartily disagree with them, I do so not on the basis that they are being unreasonable, superstitious, and irrational whereas the doctors who criticize them are not. The doctors also have a complex belief system, even though their "god" is a very different deity than that of the Christian Science parents.

As a pastor, I spend much of my day visiting people who are more victims of our health care system than the beneficiaries. Many of these people die while under the treatment of well-meaning physicians. Yet these physicians are not brought into a court for patient abuse. Why? To a great degree it is because we believe in the "god" of modern medicine whereas most Americans do not believe in the "god" represented by the Christian Science parents.

All I am arguing is that *modernity ought to be more honest about the ways in which its own criteria for determining right or wrong are context dependent.*

The Constitution of a New World

Modernity is a creation of certain stories. When we think of science, we have been taught to think of science primarily through the accounts of Louis Pasteur, Madam Curie, Copernicus, and Galileo. These have given us a well-developed mythology of the scientist struggling against the forces of ignorance—ignorance which was often supported by religion. Rarely does the mythology of modern science tell the rest of the story such as, the mighty bomb which was dropped on Japanese civilians, the uses of technology by the Nazis, and the enlistment of science in the international arms race. Stories project "worlds." Texts like scripture are *constitutive*, that is, they are busy constituting new worlds. The church is the imaginative projection of a biblical text. The Bible is not merely describing a new world but also constructing one. Being Christian is not equivalent to being a human being. A Christian is a human being who has listened to a story, such as that told of Peter's imprisonment in Acts 12. Listening to such stories makes us into peculiar people who respond to life in peculiar ways.

For instance, three decades ago a young priest in South Africa defended his black congregation against the evils of apartheid. When his people were uprooted, transported far away, and their homes bulldozed down, this young priest spoke out against the government. As a new, all-white town —named Triumph by the white residents—rose where there once had been a poor, black neighborhood, the young priest was ordered out of South Africa. His bishop supported the government's action against the young Christian "troublemaker."

Here is a story of the triumph of racism and oppression, an all too common story in our modern age.

But there was another story at work, one which we might have missed had we not been listening to Acts 12. While that young priest was standing against the South African regime, he went about his pastoral duties. He visited a young altar boy who was in the hospital with tuberculosis, an all too common disease among the poor.

The priest's name was Trevor Huddleston. The little boy's name was Desmond Tutu.

The post-modern world is an age in which old Enlightenment texts are crumbling. The lure of absolute certainty, of universal, universally applicable principles like "reason" is in demise. In such a post-modern world, we have a marvelous opportunity to again re-discover the claims of scripture. The Bible is not content to be translated into the categories of the contemporary world, but rather the Bible wants to absorb the contemporary world into its text.

The story of Peter's imprisonment, as told in Acts 12, is a story which shows every intention of going head to head with many of the dearly held assumptions of the imperial Roman world. It has similar intentions of confrontation with our own modern imperialism.

So in your church and mine, when we listen to the Bible, our primary question should not be, "How can we interpret the Bible in such a way that it makes sense to modern people?"

The Bible is not content to leave modern people as they are. It wants to convert and change them. These stories assault modern people no less than they assaulted the world view of imperial Romans. So the question is not, How can we interpret the Bible to suit the limitations in church, but, *How can we re-interpret the church to suit the demands of the Bible?*

Our congregations must read scripture out of conviction that, even as in the first centuries of our faith, the Bible is able to evoke the people it deserves.

Professor Elizabeth Achtemeier, in encouraging preachers to be more biblical in their preaching, admits that modern congregations may express surprise and even offense at hearing the ancient biblical story. "But our job is not to apologize for the scriptures," she says, "it is to preach them."

The story caused offense when it was first preached in places like Nazareth; we should not be surprised that it continues to offend. In fact, we preachers ought to be troubled when our handling of the Bible *never* offends!

Karl Barth persistently argued that the great heritage of the Enlightenment was *autonomy*, the notion of humanity as self-grounded, a race of beings who listened for no word because they did not expect to be addressed by any being other than themselves. Humanity unaddressed is a fearful entity, as the devastating results of our twentieth-century quest for human autonomy bear witness. The church exists as an outpost of expectant listening, a people being evoked by a God who refuses to be silent. The primary way of our being addressed is the Bible.

No one said that it was easy to live in this new world being created in your church by scripture, but it can certainly be an adventure.

Last summer we drove down to somewhere between Lake City and Coward, South Carolina (do you know the place?), to hear my father-in-law preach his third farewell sermon as he prepared to retire from the Christian ministry (for the third time). After his first retirement ten years ago, he was sent to a series of tiny rural churches. But this year he told the bishop that now, at last, he was positively going to retire for good and move to the mountains.

The hot Sunday sun rose over green tobacco fields as the service began in the little church. He had asked a quartet of sweet soprano voices to sing his favorite, "The Ninety-and-Nine." Do you recall the song, it's the one about the Lost Sheep: "There were ninety-and-nine, safe in the fold . . ." I don't think that I have heard it since I was a child.

After they sang, he preached. Before he set off for the mountains and retirement, Carl Parker preached. His text? Jesus' parable of the Lost Sheep. It was Father's Day, so he talked a bit about how we all love and cherish our children. God loves us even more than that, he said.

Then he began to speak about the man who was to die in the electric chair in South Carolina the next day. I had seen his picture on the news the night before. Someone had held a service of remembrance for this man's victims and their families. He had killed someone, maimed others, in his rampage of terror through the state a few years ago. The preacher at *that* service declared that he wished they would let him "throw the switch on this piece of refuse who destroyed so many innocent lives." Mr. Parker went into lurid detail describing the crimes of this man. "And yet," he said, "and yet today's scripture, as well as the sweet song we have heard, says that God loves that man on death row, and values his soul just as much as God values us."

The congregation became very quiet.

"Why, according to Jesus' little story of the Lost Sheep, God will gladly leave the ninety-and-nine gathered safe in the fold here this morning, and go up to Columbia to death row just to get hold of that one lost sheep. And when God finds him, God's more glad to have him than to have all of us safe ones here in church. Heaven goes wild when just one of these lost ones comes back home. According to Jesus."

I noted at the end of the service, that this congregation seemed a great deal more willing to let old Preacher Parker go on and retire to the mountains.

Such is the risk of being a people who have the Bible as *their book*, the stories of Jesus as *their story*.

3

The Church as the Bible's People

We have characterized the Bible as a book which has as its goal the evocation and constitution of a peculiar people—Israel and the church. You and I, in your congregation and mine, are participants in that never-ending biblical phenomenon of a people of faith being created out of nothing. Just as the Spirit moved across the waters at Creation (Genesis 1), so the Spirit descended at Pentecost (Acts 2) and created a new community where before there were only strangers.

The Bible repeatedly affirms that the word of God creates that of which it speaks. God's word is an active, effective power which brings new things into being. Psalm 33:9 celebrates this divine verbal creativity: "For he spoke, and it came to be; he commanded, and it stood forth."

Your congregation is unusual and utterly necessary, not because it does good things in the neighborhood, after all, many other worthy agencies do good things for the community. Your church is important not because the people who gather there are particularly friendly and inclusive, after all, the carefully selected crowd at the local country club are often very friendly. Your congregation is unique because it alone listens to, and attempts to order its life on the basis of the Bible.

This is us at our best.

Just three decades ago, the church in Germany went through a devastating test during the *Hitlerzeit*, the "Hitler Time." It was a test which, for the most part, the church flunked. As the great theologian Karl Barth said, when the time came for the German church to stand up and say "No!" it was about two hundred years too late, having said "Yes" to so much. The greatest theological minds of the German church were enlisted to convince the church that the greatest task of contemporary Christians is to understand and to communicate with the "modern world." But in leaning over to speak to this brave new "modern world," the church fell in. The church had at last succeeded in such a way as to be understood and accepted not only by Copernicus and Darwin, but also by the Nazis.

Karl Barth was horrified that the church lacked the theological resources to stand against Hitler. But having spent decades convinced that the Bible was just one book among many, that the Jewishness of Jesus was not really all that important, that the test of Christianity is how well it undergirds the aspirations of the nation, that the tradition of the church is little more than the forward development and eventual merging of all the world's great religions, there was nothing left wherewith to make a stand. The church had lost the means to resist, had lost the means even to know that there was something worth resisting.

Jesus was not really a Jew, they had said. The important thing about Jesus was that he exemplified the best and the brightest of all human aspiration. He was the teacher of noble human ideals. It was a short step from the liberal Christ-the-highest-in-humanity to the Nazi Superman.

But there were some in the German church who remembered. In 1934 Karl Barth wrote the Barmen Declaration. It began:

> *Jesus Christ, as he is attested for us in Holy Scripture, is the one Word of God which we have to hear and which we have to trust in life and in death.*
> *We reject as false doctrine [that the church] . . . would have to acknowledge as a source of its proclamation apart from and besides this one Word of God, still other events, powers, figures and truths, as God's revelation.*

See? When the church was bereft of leaders, power, protection, only one thing was left for us. The word of God, thank God, remained, calling forth a new Confessing Church in Germany, as if from nothing. Time and again in our history, the word of God has evoked the church it deserved, thus fulfilling the prophetic promise, "My word . . . shall not return to me empty, but it shall accomplish that which I purpose, and succeed in the thing for which I sent it." (Isaiah 55:11)

Peter Storey, Methodist Bishop in South Africa, tireless crusader against the evils of apartheid, says that no decisions in the church matter as much as the church's decision to speak and to live by God's truth. If the church wavers on that, then nothing we do means anything.

God's truth is a matter of being willing to be confronted, convicted, and corrected by the Bible.

As modern people, we have often been taught to believe that the answers to life's issues lie within us. Education has its goal to "lead out" an answer from within us. *Educare* is pointed out as the root of "education." The assumption is that we have within ourselves the resources to know and to articulate the truth. On the other hand, the Bible moves from the assumption that the normative articulations of faith lie outside the individual human psyche, wait for us, are given to us as a gift. The biblical canon asserts, by its very existence, that it is not right for us to live in chaos, in narcissistic subjectivity. We are not left to our own devices:

> Keep these words that I am commanding
> you today in your heart. Recite them to your

children and talk about them when you are at home and when you are away, when you lie down and when you rise. (Deuteronomy 6:6-7)

A strong culture expends a great deal of time keeping its stories straight. Certain texts will be identified as classics. The classic texts will be familiar to anyone in the culture and a great deal of effort will be put forth in instructing and initiating the young into these texts. Even as the culture expends a great deal of effort keeping the classic texts straight in its own consciousness, these classic texts function to help keep the culture straight about who it is and where it ought to be going.

When Martin Luther King, Jr. stood before the Lincoln Memorial and quoted our nation's Declaration of Independence, he was citing a classic national text, one known by heart by everyone there. Yet it was a text whose vision was awaiting full realization. King said, in effect, "You have said in your own founding documents, 'All are created equal.' Now is the time to live by our originating text or else remain ridiculously out-of-step with our own texts."

All of this will sound familiar to you because it happens quite often in the congregation—a people being confronted by their book.

Let Us Tell You a Story

The primary biblical way of knowing is through story. When questions arise in the church, we have no other way of responding to those questions other than by first telling a story. This is the primary and characteristic mode of knowledge for biblical people. Certainly, there are many biblical texts which do not appear to be narrative in nature. But even these texts are story-dependent, that is, biblical assertions and propositions (when they rarely occur) are themselves story dependent.

For instance, we read in Deuteronomy the Ten Commandments which Moses received on Mt. Sinai. From time to time people have tried to put forth these Ten Commandments as universal laws which were applicable to everyone in society. But such a move does an injustice to the nature of the Ten Commandments. The Commandments themselves arise out of story, a story of a God who came for us when we were slaves in Egypt and delivered us. "You have seen what I did to the Egyptians, and how I bore you on eagles' wings and brought you to myself." (Exodus 19:4-6)

Why did God deliver us? The story says that Moses begged Pharaoh to let the Hebrew children go because they had been commanded to worship God. Pharaoh resisted, but after ten plagues, he finally relented. Then the children of Israel were free to go and worship God out in the wilderness. How does this people worship God? Israel worships God by following certain commandments which are given by God. Now this may strike the outside observer as a peculiar way to worship: you shall not steal, you shall not commit adultery, you shall not bear false witness. But Israel has a peculiar God who demands a peculiar kind of worship.

The justification therefore for the Ten Commandments is not that they are universally applicable, or that if everyone followed them, society would move along much better. The biblical justification for the Ten Commandments is that these are ways in which a people delivered by God out of Egyptian slavery respond to that God. The Commandments are the means by which a peculiar community is created by a peculiar God who wants a family. Generally speaking, we do injustice to most biblical material when we try to make it universally or individually applicable. The Bible speaks to that peculiar people who are evoked by this strange, wonderful story of a God "who brought you out of the land of Egypt, out of the house of slavery" (Exodus 20:3).

In reading biblical stories we note a number of characteristics of story which have implications for the life of the church.

Stories tend to be concrete. They are rarely concerned with universal truths but rather with specific, particular details. *Stories are flexible and open ended.* They will have many different levels of meaning, far too many images to be pursued at any one time. The richness of story means that they are always open-ended. *Stories are never finished*, but constantly move and change and reveal new levels of meaning in every telling.

Stories tend to be a catalyst for our imagination. Unlike limited, abstract propositions, stories tend to multiply our options. They show the rich array of divine and human response to any situation. They continually remind us that the future is not closed and fixed, but always thick with possibility. *Stories are experiential.* In listening to a story, we find ourselves deeply engaged in it. Our experiences relate to the experiences being depicted in the story. We find ourselves much more involved in listening to a story than we are when listening to simple propositions. Finally, *stories tend to be communal in nature.* It takes two to story. Human solidarity is enhanced in listening to stories. Moreover, stories are often an exchange between the generations, the old initiating the young.

In listening to the stories of the Bible, we are making available to the listener a new identity. "And when in the future your child asks you, 'What does this mean?' You shall say to him . . . ." (Exodus 13:14)

Poetry as Politics

Much of the Bible is story and a great deal of it is poetry. Be careful with such poetry. It is more than just sweet, religious thoughts. It has a subversive political function. By singing the Bible's songs, an old, established order is being dismantled and a new order is being put in its place. The mighty are being brought low and the wretched of the earth are being lifted up. People who were nobodies are being formed into somebodies.

At the beginning of Luke's Gospel, a number of people began singing. An old couple up at the Temple, Elizabeth and Zechariah, are met by the angel of God and they sing. Mary, a young, unmarried peasant woman is greeted by God's messenger and she sings:

> My soul magnifies the Lord,
>   and my spirit rejoices in God my Savior.
> (Luke 1:47)

This is no lullaby! The words thunder forth like a battle chant:

> He has shown strength with his arm; he has scattered the proud in the thoughts of their hearts. He has brought down the powerful from their thrones; and lifted up the lowly. (Luke 1:51-52)

Not too sweet a Christmas carol. It's a song about someone low going up, someone up high being brought low. You won't hear women singing like this except in Soweto, Warsaw, Harlem, or South Chicago. When God makes a move into history, voiceless people who have had nothing but dirges on their lips, break into song. A couple of years ago, the government in Praetoria banned the lighting of candles or the singing of Christmas carols in Soweto. When the press asked

why, the South African Scrooge replied, "You
know how emotional black women are. Christmas
carols have an emotional effect upon them" (*St.
Louis Post-Dispatch*, Dec. 27, 1985). If you let a poor
Jewish woman like Mary sing, or a black mother in
Soweto sing, you don't know where it might lead.

Imagine first-century Judea in the December
darkness, without a star in the sky, with people
shut up in the darkened houses for fear of Roman
soldiers, the streets deserted and fearfully quiet.
(One way to handle an oppressive situation in a
place like Nazareth is to keep your head down,
your mouth buttoned shut.) There, in the dark
silence, a pure, clear, feminine voice cuts through
the night.

> My soul magnifies the Lord, . . .
> He has brought down the powerful from their
> thrones,
> and lifted up the lowly.

Before Herod knows what's happening, the
streets are full of chanting, restless people on the
move.

It is important to see that biblical poetry is
making a political claim. The primary mode of
governmental communication is prose. Prose
keeps things tied down, prohibits flights of fancy
or leaps of the imagination. Prose reports the
world as fixed, settled, factual, something to be
accepted rather than questioned. In opposition to

such establishmentarian ways of speaking, biblical language is busy lifting us above the prosaic world of the now, dismantling an old order and helping us to participate, if now only through the poetic, in a very new and different world.

When Martin Luther King, Jr. gave his "I Have a Dream" speech, he was speaking poetically. He was dreaming. But his dreams were not wishful thinking about what might be. Through his speech, his poetic evocation of a new reality, he was constructing that new reality. This often happens in the Bible. Through prophetic poetry, the presumptive world of the status quo is being called into question. Language, particularly poetic language, has a political function. Through language we legitimate or delegitimate configurations of power.

Many liberal Christians are turned off by apocalyptic speech, talk about the end of the world, such as we find in biblical books like The Book of Daniel and Revelation. They see talk of the end of time as simply "pie in the sky by and by" theology which keeps people enslaved to present conditions rather than equipping them to rise above their circumstances. This assessment of apocalyptic speech is wrong headed. Apocalyptic speech is always a prelude to biblical revolution. Many of Jesus' pronouncements were apocalyptic in nature, an announcement of the end. The end must be announced before there can be a new beginning. We must have some credible vision of the future before we can let go of the present. We must have confidence that the future is God's before we are willing to step out of the past. Bible talk about the end of the present order, such as we find in the Book of Revelation, is politically sensitive material. The known world and those who profit from present social and political arrangements cannot tolerate speech about the end of the world. Speech about the end of the world is not an escape from the world, but rather a prophetic engagement with visionary thinking in order that new reality might break through.

Sometimes we say of our preachers, "She is a real prophet." Too often what we mean is that this preacher is adept in the art of scolding, moralizing, and judgmental diatribe. Prophets are carping social critics who take on controversial issues from the pulpit. While biblical prophets were definitely controversial, the source of their controversy was usually their poetry rather than their radical posturing. They continually called and recalled Israel to be Israel; to return and remember who they were as God's holy people. Through story, parable, and poetry, these biblical prophets attempted to call the people back to their original story which had given birth to Israel as a people. In this sense Jesus was a prophet when he preached at Nazareth in Luke 4. He used our familiar story to recall us to our true identity. Prophets, biblical prophets, are engaged in a dispute over what is possible. Through their speech, they disrupt the old consensus, and pave the way for a new community based not upon what works, or the present consensus, but rather upon the workings and will of God.

All of this is to remind us that Israel told its stories as a conscious political act in order carefully to define themselves against the cultures of their day. Early Christians told their stories in order to set themselves over against the imperial emperor-worshiping court of Rome. Through these texts they both drew the line between themselves and the Empire, and projected themselves into a fresh future that would not have been known had God not spoken it to them.

> How beautiful upon the mountains
>   are the feet of the messenger who an-
>   nounces peace,
> who brings good news,
>   who announces salvation,
> who says to Zion, "Your God reigns." (Isaiah
> 52:7)

In discussing the political, community-forming nature of biblical story, Walter Brueggemann says:

> Israel's narrative is a partisan, polemical narrative. It is concerned to build a counter community—counter to the oppression of Egypt, counter to the seduction of Canaan, counter to every cultural alternative and every imperial pretense. There is nothing in this narrative that will appeal to outsiders who

belong to another consensus, or who share a different ethos and participate in another epistemology. To such persons, Israel's narratives are silly, narrow, scandalous, and obscurantist. . . . Torah intends to nurture insiders who are willing to risk a specific universe of discourse and cast their lot there. . . . Shall we risk these stories? Shall we take our stand on them? . . . The answer is known only when we decide if we want to subvert the imperial consciousness and offer a genuine alternative to the dominant forms of power, value, and knowledge. (*The Creative Word*, Fortress Press, 1982, p. 27)

It thus makes a great deal of difference how the church speaks, how we sing Zion's songs in a strange land. Our congregation is being shaped, for good or ill, through the words we use in our worship and work together. It is therefore a matter of life or death for the congregation when we substitute other language—the talk of psychology, the speech of sociology, economics, or good old American consumerism—for the speech of Israel and church.

I am concerned, for instance, by the music of our worship, It is incumbent upon the congregation to criticize the way in which it prays and praises. Who is the God whom we are praising? In contemporary "Christian" music I hear songs about Jesus the good friend, Jesus the lover who builds us up, affirms us, supports us, but not too much about Jesus who makes demands upon us. People come away from worship on Sunday morning, after being exposed to such drivel, feeling a bit better, having a vague sense of having participated in some sort of spiritual "high," but not at all sure of any counter cultural claim having been made on their lives.

The response to such criticism is often, "Well, it's not great music, to be sure. But the people like it. They seem to get a blessing from it. And we have got to be sensitive to the needs of people."

I am unmoved by such rationalizations. The church is not in the business of "blessing" people, existing as just another agency to fulfill people's desires. The church is a school of desire, teaching us what things are worth wanting, what desires are worth fulfilling. The church, and the story to which it is accountable, has some very definite ideas about the goal of life, the purpose of human existence. The worship in your church is not just another narcotic in an anesthetizing culture. The worship of the church is our attempt to listen to God. We begin with the assumption that many of us are in pain today, drifting, unhappy, unfulfilled, not because we have not tried to find pleasure, direction, happiness and satisfaction, Lord knows, we've tried. We are miserable because we have been looking for fulfillment in the wrong places, fulfilling our hungers with cheap nourishment, attempting to base our lives on lies rather than on truth. We come to church empty and numb.

It really is tough out there for our people. They

face challenges, questions, horrible tragedies. How insensitive of us to respond to their pain with cheap substitutes for real salvation. How calloused of us to send them forth unarmed, unaided in their quest for meaning and significance in life. What a shame when Sunday dribbles off into easy platitudes and soothing generalities when the Bible could have helped us to name the pain and to sign our way into new reality.

> Make the mind of this people dull,
>   and stop their ears,
>   and shut their eyes,
> so that they may not look with their eyes,
>   and listen with their ears,
> and comprehend with their minds,
>   and turn and be healed. (Isaiah 6:10)

The church is the Bible's people. We are the only listeners God has got. So we ought to examine our Sunday worship, the content of our sermons, the substance of our prayers and songs, the purpose of our meetings, the priorities of our budgets with an eye to how well these congregational activities help us to listen for God's word. For it is in his word, as he guides and teaches us, that we are met by our best hope.

"As he went ashore, he saw a great crowd; and he had compassion for them, because they were like sheep without a shepherd; and he began to teach them many things" (Mark 6:34).

4

Formed and Ever Reformed by the Bible

We believe that the synagogue—that place of worship where Jesus went in Nazareth, where they handed him the scroll and he stood up to speak with such memorable results—has its roots in Israel's time of exile. What do you do when you're a "stranger in a strange land"? How does one cope with being a resident alien in a culture which ignores the God of Israel?

We gather. We set aside time from our daily cares, not to escape, but to engage, to focus ourselves on what matters, to rise above the many distractions of life within the Empire in order that we might again be able to name the name, tell the old story, sing the old gospel songs, stand before The Book.

By the rivers of Babylon—there we sat down
and there we wept
when we remembered Zion. . . .
For there our captors asked us for songs,
and our tormentors asked for mirth, saying,
"Sing us one of the songs of Zion!"
How could we sing the LORD'S song
in a foreign land?
If I forget you, O Jerusalem,
let my right hand wither! (Psalm 137:1-5)

How shall we sing the Lord's song in a strange land? That has been the congregational question for Israel and the church ever since our beginning. And from the beginning, it was the Word, the recalled, remembered, recreative Word which kept us going.

It is the same for your congregation today.

As frequently noted throughout this book, this Word among us is no merely confirming, comforting word. The Bible is not only forming us but also reforming us, making us over, over and over again, into people who more closely resemble the family whom God's righteousness demands.

Conversation overheard on Parent's Weekend on our campus:

"Well, your son is twenty-one. It must be great to at last be done with him."

"I can tell you have never been a mother," said the other person. "I will not be done with him until I die."

Fortunately for the church, God is not yet done with us.

Ways the Bible Forms the Congregation

Let us be clear that, as Christians, we do not believe in congregating together for togetherness' sake. According to the Bible, human beings may be brought together for a variety of purposes, many of them in direct opposition to the reign of God. We act out our sinfulness as well in community as in solitude; sometimes, as Reinhold Niebuhr stated, we are often more immoral in community than when we are alone.

"Come, let us build ourselves a city, and a tower with its top in the heavens, and let us make a name for ourselves; otherwise we shall be scattered abroad" (Genesis 11:4), we said to ourselves at Babel. This, so far as we know, was the first instance of international cooperation. We simply could not stand to be under God.

"Here comes this dreamer. Come now, let us kill him," we said in response to the dreams of little brother Joseph (Genesis 37:20), huddling together against the one who was different from our community.

"The people gathered themselves together to Aaron, and said to him, 'Make gods for us'"

(Exodus 32:1), uniting in our desire to have gods more to our liking than the God we got in Yahweh.

"But they all cried out together, 'Away with this fellow! Release Barabbas for us. . . . They shouted out, 'Crucify, crucify him!'" (Luke 23:18-21), demonstrating the fruits of democracy in action against the one sent to save us.

In a society in which widespread loneliness is almost a necessary byproduct of those who value individual freedom above all else, many people are in a desperate search for "community." Many of them will come to the church. Mistakenly, they understand the church as just another human gathering, more dedicated to friendliness than truthfulness. To make matters worse, many congregations, lacking any certainty about the theological purposes of the church and its mission, peddle the idea of community based upon ethnic, economic, or sociological similarity. Church becomes little more than another gathering with people just like me. "Community," untested by any criterion other than our need to huddle in groups, can be demonic.

It has long been a Christian belief that we have no better means of preserving our congregations from the more demonic effects of perverted community than our confrontation with the Bible. The Bible not only forms us but also judges us and therefore reforms us. In your church and mine, we are constantly being examined by scripture, the same way Jesus allowed the scripture of the community to critique the inadequacy of community in Nazareth (Luke 4).

We assemble for church, the choir and clergy are in place, the organ blares forth, and we all sit in orderly rows of pews. This is the congregation at worship. And all might go well were it not for the intrusive prophetic Word:

> Hear the word of the LORD. . . . When you stretch out your hands, I will hide my eyes from you; even though you make many prayers, I will not listen; your hands are full of blood. Wash yourselves; make yourselves clean; remove the evil of your doings from before my eyes; cease to do evil, learn to do good; seek justice, rescue the oppressed, defend the orphan, plead for the widow. (Isaiah 1:10, 15-17)

It is this Word, coming upon us, assaulting, reforming us, which makes a congregation *Christian*.

The Bible confronts the congregation in the following ways:

Preaching. Preaching is biblical whenever the preacher allows a biblical text to serve as the major means of shaping the content and purpose of the sermon. Preaching is at its best when the preacher stands up and tells the truth about what happens when a biblical text intersects our lives and makes a claim upon us. Such preaching isn't easy, perhaps that is why we hear so little of it. Biblical preaching takes a lifetime of wrestling with the Bible, acquiring skills of interpretation, methods of careful listening. It also takes a lifetime with the congregation, listening to the people who are listening to the Bible.

Most of the work a pastor does on a biblical sermon is invisible. The congregation cannot know the time, the agony, the struggle expended by the pastor in producing that twenty-minute sermon. Perhaps that is one reason why many ministers, torn between so many worthy pastoral activities, forsake the preaching task and make do with less than the congregation expects from the pulpit.

The Bible in the Church

Burton H. Throckmorton, Jr., a distinguished biblical scholar writing in *The Christian Century*, typifies the homiletical neglect of the Bible in too many contemporary congregations:

Having participated in worship in many different places in recent years, I have been increasingly struck by the fact that the Bible has become almost totally irrelevant. With some notable exceptions, the scripture readings do not even begin to illuminate the

87

sermons; occasionally there are not even any such reading, but if there are they are promptly forgotten. In very few instances have sermons functioned as the means of illuminating the Word of God.

Occasionally one finds a formal, superficial connection between scripture and sermon, as though one has done one's duty by referring at some point in to a previously read selection of scripture; but any wrestling with a biblical text to extract from it some bit of light on one's life and the community's life under God is almost never visible. Most sermons state either the obvious or the ridiculous, and are not to be compared in substance or insight with the op-ed page of a first-rate newspaper. When I go to church I long to hear a Word from God—not another commentary on the current scene or, worse yet, a series of banalities. But I usually find that the Bible is not thought to raise any questions about life, to provide any nourishment for it, to make any promises to it.

Contemporary congregations must give their preachers the time and encouragement they need to preach biblically. With the new Common Lectionary and its many printed resources there are more aids for the biblical preacher than ever before. We simply must demand that our preachers do business with the Bible.

Pastoral Care. How to be deeply concerned for and yet utterly free of other people? That is the dilemma for most pastors today. We live in a therapeutic culture which values good feelings more than good living. We live in a consumeristic culture whose main goal is the fulfillment of personal desire, with absolutely no limit upon our desires. This can be a dangerous environment for the pastor who characterizes his or her main function as "caring for people."

The Bible appears to know little of the psychologization of human nature or the concomitant therapeutic manipulation of people. Self-esteem is not a biblical concern. The Bible's disinterest in such activities is not only because the Bible is a very old book but, also, because it is a very truthful one. It asserts that we will not get better until we become more faithful. Discipleship is its goal more than therapy.

The Bible depicts a form of existence, discipleship, which is not primarily about health or wholeness. We are called to faithfulness, which often entails suffering, rejection, and pain. If we can be healthy or whole in the process, so much the better, but whether we feel good about ourselves or not God cares for us by giving us something more interesting to live for than ourselves.

So one of the Bible's chief functions within the congregation is giving content to our care, setting the limits upon our efforts to help people. Lacking such content or limits, we usually opt for whatever secular therapy happens to be in vogue and offer that as Christian care.

Christian Education. The Bible is an ancient, foreign book. It is foreign not only in language, thought patterns, and cultural origins but also in its approach to reality. Contemporary congregations, schooled in the culture of the Enlightenment, must go through a cultural shift in order fully to enter the world of the Bible.

Therefore, the church can expect to expend great time and energy in its dealings with the Bible. We are, in effect, asking people to learn a new language, enter a new culture in order to hear the testimony of scripture.

I predict that the contemporary church will find itself expending increasing efforts in teaching. Mainline Christianity often assumed that there was no great disjunction between the church and the world. After all, we were fortunate enough to have been born into a "Christian" nation. Our young became Christian merely by drinking the water and breathing the air. Being Christian was something akin to being American. One did not need intensive education and formation in such an environment. All one needed was gentle nurture and encouragement to be true to the best already present in the self.

If we were ever justified in thinking this way, we are no longer justified today. Increasing numbers of American Christians are sensing the discord between the Christian faith and our surrounding culture. In this environment, images of conversion replace images of nurture. People come to their religious gatherings looking for equipment to resist the world, rather than the means to adapt to the world. Christian education takes on new significance.

Every congregation ought carefully to examine the way it educates its people for discipleship. Are we giving them enough equipment to resist? What is happening to our young people? In this book we have often spoken of the distance or the gap between us and the Bible. On the other side, are we giving our people enough knowledge about the Bible to enable them to be relatively at home with it? Through ignorance of the Bible, have we made it so alien to them that it is utterly beyond their comprehension?

My neighbor, the Rabbi at the synagogue, expects to spend the better part of his week teaching. After all, his people must not only learn Hebrew but then must use their Hebrew in reading scripture. Perhaps of even greater significance for their religious education, they must be Jews in a world that seems to have no place for Jews. Teaching scripture is a life-and-death matter for Jews.

I predict that the North American Protestant church will begin to resemble the synagogue in its educational use of scripture.

Prayer and Worship. We live in a very utilitarian

environment, part of our Enlightenment heritage, where everything is valued on the basis of its instrumentality, how well it helps us in getting what we want. The Bible asserts that prayer and worship are primarily means of getting what God wants. Worship, therefore, is not about buttressing personal morality, not about inducing a spiritual high to make us feel better, nor primarily about motivating us for social action. Worship is about being encountered by a holy God.

We have already spoken about the need to be concerned with the content of our worship, prayer, and praise. While we are praising God, we are, for good or ill, being formed as the church. Are we being malformed by ideologies which subvert biblical reality? Is there enough liturgical richness to equip God's people to withstand the challenges they will face next week? Is our worship a complex act of avoidance of God rather than confrontation with God?

Sunday worship is the primary occasion for most of us to be confronted by the Bible. The Bible was written to be read orally, in public, in the congregation's assembly. Increased exposure to the riches of scripture is a primary agenda for the contemporary church on Sunday morning.

Ethics. People are changed, not by ethical urging but by transformed imagination. Poetic vision is catalytic to prophetic action. Ministry becomes misery when it is nothing more than protecting a congregation from the truth of the gospel. Church too easily slips into a conspiracy of deception which attempts to keep the dominant values of our culture credible rather than assaulting those values from a biblical perspective. Human hurt and human hope are evaded with talk of adjustment and accommodation. Prophets are those who inevitably use language "to pluck up and to pull down, to destroy and overthrow" (Jeremiah 1:10) so that something new might come. The language of the Bible is fundamentally prophetic, always inviting us to deep conflict with conventional, establishment visions of reality.

Much of the ethical clout of the Bible is indirect, secondary, derivative rather than immediate. Sometimes the Bible comes forward with simple, clear admonitions for human behavior. More often though, ethics is a secondary enterprise for the Bible, a human byproduct of the primary biblical task of depicting a living and just God. The Bible seems to assume that, if it can get us looking in the right direction, then we shall act accordingly. We can only live in a world we can see.

Church Administration. Are you surprised that this topic should be included here? For many pastors, administration of the congregation is the most onerous of pastoral duties, mundane drudgery. Yet in administration, we are forming the congregation, caring for those daily matters which keep a church together. The Bible does not despise the earthly, the humanly; in fact, it redeems the mundane and the ordinary, depicting everyday matters as of divine consequence. An ordinary church meeting (Acts 11:1-18) can become a divine-human meeting.

When church leaders merely ape secular administrators, something significant is lost for the church. The Bible reminds us that all our meeting, deliberating, mailing, organizing has as its ultimate goal the turning of our congregation toward God. Time and again in our life together, the Bible will be able to cut through our organizational insulation and call us out of mere bureaucracy toward church. Time and again the Bible is able to reopen the God question for an acculturated church, revealing our organizing structures as idolatrous facsimiles rather than church. The Bible sets our organizational agenda, encouraging us to seek fidelity more than efficiency, conversion more than stability.

In the Bible, our little, ordinary lives are lifted up and given cosmic significance. We come to see ourselves, and the everyday dealings within our congregations, as part of a great journey with God. Such a vision makes church administration worth doing.

Social Action. I am convinced that only the Bible offers the church the power to rise above the status quo in society. Without the Bible we have no way of conceiving of a new heaven and new earth, much less how to get there. Someone must speak to us of a God who unsettles present social arrangements in order to form a new people.

"Blessed are you who weep now, for you will laugh . . . Woe to you who are laughing now, for you will mourn and weep." (Luke 6:21, 25)

Lacking an apocalyptic vision of newness, pastors can do little more than be therapeutic.

> They have treated the wound of my people
> carelessly,
> saying, "Peace, peace,"
> when there is no peace.
>
> (Jeremiah 6:14; 8:11)

Psychic numbing sets in and we come to accept injustice as the status quo. The modern, democratic nation/state is far from being a benign fellow traveler for the church. As we noted in the early sections of this book, modernity is powerful competition for the gospel.

We must let go before we can move on.

God's primary means of moving on is the church. Elsewhere I have argued, with Stanley Hauerwas, that the main social policy of the church is the church; that is, the church is the present, visible means of organizing humanity (*Resident Aliens*, Abingdon Press, 1989). When the church is asked to say something political, the first thing we ought to say is "church," that is, a human congregation based not on violence but on peace, not on ethnic, economic, or social factors but on God's vocation. The visible, countercultural alternative to the modern nation with its institutionalized self-interest, its propensity for violence, and its arrogant claims is the church.

The church's social action mandate is more radical than giving a little advice to congress or doing a few nice things to keep a lid on our town. The church's mandate is to be formed by God into a people who are visibly, distinctively different in their lives together, to be light and salt for a dying world. In the church we are to pioneer those social structures which the world, in its myopic vision, has not even thought of yet. We believe the world lacks the resources to organize itself upon any other principle than selfishness or violence because it has not been given the means to be both truthful and peaceful.

Our chief means of being truthful is exposure to the Bible.

And what invigorating, frightening, revitalizing exposure it can be!

> The voice of the Lord is powerful;
>   the voice of the Lord is full of majesty.
> The voice of the Lord breaks the cedars;
>   the Lord breaks the cedars of Lebanon. . . .
> The voice of the Lord causes the oaks to whirl,
>   and strips the forest bare;
>   and in his temple all say, "Glory!"
> May the LORD bless his people with peace!
>   (Psalm 29:4-5, 9, 11)